W9-AAX-470

AMERICA AT WAR

WORLD WAR II

JOHN PERRITANO

Library of Congress Cataloging-in-Publication Data

Perritano, John.

World War II / [John Perritano].

p. cm. — (America at war)

Includes index.

ISBN 0-531-23211-5/978-0-531-23211-8/ (hardcover)

1. World War, 1939-1945—Juvenile literature. I. Title.
II. Title: World War Two. III. Title: World War 2.

D743.7.P47 2010

940.53--dc22

2010035050

This edition published by
Scholastic Inc., 557 Broadway; New York, NY

SCHOLASTIC, FRANKLIN WATTS, and associated logos are
trademarks and/or registered trademarks of Scholastic Inc.

232654 10/10

Printed in Heshan City, China
10 9 8 7 6 5 4 3 2 1

Created by Q2AMedia
www.q2amedia.com

Text, design & illustrations Copyright © Q2AMedia 2011

Editor Jessica Cohn   **Senior Designer** Rahul Dhiman
Publishing Director Chester Fisher   **Project Manager** Kunal Mehrotra
Client Service Manager Santosh Vasudevan   **Art Editor** Sujatha Menon
Art Director Joita Das   **Picture Researcher** Debobrata Sen

Picture Credits

t=top b=bottom c=center l=left r=right
m=middle

Cover Images: Front (All): DNational
Archives and Records Administration,
Tsgt Ben Bloker: U.S.Air Force.

Back: Joe Rosenthal: National Archives
and Records Administration.

Half Title: National Archives and
Records Administration.

Content Page: AP Photo.

4 National Archives and Records
Administration. 5t Library of Congress
Prints and Photographs Division
Washington, D.C. 20540 USA.
5b Farm Security Administration:
Office of War Information Black-and-
White Negatives: Library of Congress.
6-7 AP Photo. 8-9 AP Photo.
10-11 AP Photo. 12-13 AP Photo.
15l AP Photo. 15r New Times Paris
Bureau Collection. (USIA): National
Archives and Records Administration.
16-17 AP Photo. 17t AP Photo.
18-19 National Archives and Records
Administration. 20-21 National
Archives and Records Administration.
20t Tsgt Ben Bloker: U.S.Air Force.

21t National Archives and Records
Administration. 22-23 National
Archives and Records Administration.
22 Joe Rosenthal: National Archives
and Records Administration. 24-25
U.S. Coast Guard: AP Photo. 25t Eddie
Worth: AP Photo. 26-27 Lt. A. E.
Samuelson. (Army): National Archives
and Records Administration. 28-29 AP
photo. 30-31 Joe Rosenthal: National
Archives and Records Administration.

Q2AMedia Art Bank: 5bl, 22t.

CONTENTS

Germany **invaded** Poland on September 1, 1939. This was the start of World War II.

The fighting ended six years later, in 1945. Over 72 million people had lost their lives. Many nations were in ruins.

The seeds of World War II were planted after World War I (1914–1918). Some people called World War I (WWI) the "War to End All Wars." But that was not the case. The United States was **allies** with Britain and France in WWI. They defeated Germany and those who sided with the Germans. After the war, many people on the winning side wanted the peace to last. Many other people, however, wanted **revenge**.

Treaty of Revenge

Revenge began with the peace **treaty** that ended World War I. That agreement was called the Treaty of Versailles. It was named for the city where the heads of state met to punish Germany for starting WWI. The treaty took away Germany's overseas **colonies**. It forced three million German-speaking people to become part of a new country called Czechoslovakia. The treaty reduced Germany's army. It forced the Germans to pay billions of dollars in war damages.

The treaty angered many Germans. One was a young German named Adolf Hitler. He vowed to return the German "Fatherland" to its former glory.

Warring Nations:

Axis: Germany, Italy, Japan
Allies: Britain, China, France, Soviet Union, United States

Leaders:

Germany: Adolf Hitler
Great Britain: Winston Churchill
Italy: Benito Mussolini
Japan: Hideki Tojo
Soviet Union: Joseph Stalin
United States: Franklin Roosevelt

Top Generals:

Admiral Isoroku Yamamoto: Japan
Field Marshal Bernard Montgomery: Great Britain
Field Marshal Irwin Rommel: Germany
Gen. Dwight D. Eisenhower: United States

Adolf Hitler

Europe on the Eve of WWII

Axis-aligned
Allies-aligned
Neutral

ICELAND (Denmark)
ATLANTIC OCEAN
SWEDEN
FINLAND
NORWAY
ESTONIA
LATVIA
LITHUANIA
UNION OF SOVIET SOCIALIST REPUBLICS
NORTHERN IRELAND
GREAT BRITAIN
DENMARK
EAST PRUSSIA (Germany)
IRELAND
ENGLAND
NETHERLANDS
BELGIUM
GERMANY
POLAND
LUXEMBOURG
SLOVAKIA
FRANCE
AUSTRIA
HUNGARY
ROMANIA
SWITZERLAND
ANDORRA
YUGOSLAVIA
BULGARIA
ARMENIA
Caspian Sea
IRAN
PORTUGAL
CORSICA (France)
ITALY
ALBANIA
TURKEY
SPAIN
SARDINIA (Italy)
GREECE
SYRIA (France)
IRAQ
SPANISH MOROCCO
ALGERIA (France)
TUNISIA (France)
MALTA (Britain)
CYPRUS (Gt. Britain)
LEBENON (France)
PALESTINE (Britain)

Joseph Stalin

invaded—entered by force

allies— friends during a time of conflict

revenge—punishment for something

treaty—agreement

colonies—groups that settle in distant lands but remain part of the country they came from

THE RISE OF HITLER

Adolph Hitler was born on April 20, 1889, in Austria. He dropped out of high school when he was 16. Hitler wanted to be an artist, but failed.

Hitler joined the German army when World War I began. The German **economy** was in trouble at the end of the war. Germany's money was worthless. Millions of people were out of work. Hitler believed the time was right for a **revolution**—a revolution he would lead.

Nazi Party

Hitler formed the National Socialist German Workers' Party in 1920. The party became known as the Nazi Party. Hitler tried to take over the government in 1923. He failed, and spent nine months in prison. During that time, he wrote a book called *Mein Kampf* (My Struggle). His book explained his political views. "Those who want to live, let them fight, and those who do not want to fight … do not deserve to live," Hitler wrote.

After he left prison, Hitler rebuilt the Nazi Party. The Nazis were **fascists**. Fascism is a system of government in which power is given to a **dictator**. Hitler became Germany's leader in 1933. He rose to power by blaming Jews and **communists** for Germany's troubles. The Nazis passed a series of laws against German Jews. Many Jews were victims of Nazi violence.

Hitler got rid of people who tried to stand in his way. He declared the Nazis the only political party in Germany.

Adolf Hitler speaks to a crowd of Germans.

economy—system of wealth and production

revolution—an overthrow of government

fascists—those who believe in fascism, or governments run by dictators

dictator—leader who rules with absolute power

communists—those who believe in communism, or government in which individuals do not own property

FASCISM ON THE MARCH

The Great Depression was a breakdown of business around the world. Banks closed. People could not find work. The Depression began in 1929 and lasted until the late 1930s. It made life difficult. Fascist governments formed in Italy and Spain as a result.

The military controlled the government in Japan. Japan's economy suffered during the Great Depression, too. The island nation had little or no **natural resources** of its own. It had to depend on **imports** from other countries.

Targeting China

Japan's leaders decided to force its Asian neighbors into a "Co-Prosperity Sphere." The nations within that sphere were forced to give Japan raw materials, such as oil. In this way, Japan got what it needed to survive. In the meantime, Japan built up its military. It created one of the strongest navies in the world.

Japan invaded the northern Chinese province of Manchuria in 1931. The Japanese set up a new nation they called Manchukuo. Japan invaded China in 1937.

The Japanese invaded Manchuria in 1931. ▶

Italy and Germany

Italy was being run by the dictator Benito Mussolini. He ordered his army to invade Abyssinia (now Ethiopia). Mussolini wanted to create an empire of his own. Elsewhere, Hitler ordered troops into the Saarland. That was an area that the Allies had taken from Germany after World War I. Hitler and Mussolini signed a treaty known as the Rome-Berlin Axis **pact**. That pact would later include Japan.

natural resources—wealth supplied by nature, such as land for farming

imports—goods brought in from other countries

pact—agreement between nations

Adolf Hitler grew bolder. He ignored the rules of the Treaty of Versailles. He rebuilt Germany's army and navy. He killed or put in prison anyone who opposed him.

Crowds line up to ▶ see the Nazi soldiers parade on the streets.

In 1938, the Nazis invaded Austria, which is Germany's neighbor. Hitler then wanted to occupy the Sudetenland. That was an area in Czechoslovakia where three million German-speaking people lived. Hitler threatened to go to war on their behalf. Another war in Europe seemed likely.

"Peace for Our Time"

British Prime Minister Neville Chamberlain held a meeting with Hitler. Chamberlain hoped to prevent another bloody conflict. Britain and France gave Hitler what he wanted on September 29, 1938. They signed an agreement that said they would not help Czechoslovakia if Germany invaded. Chamberlain returned to England. He announced that there would be "peace for our time." This manner of dealing with Hilter was known as **appeasement**. It kept the peace for only a brief period.

Poland Next?

Hitler believed France and Great Britain would back down as the Nazis marched across Europe. He was right. Nations fell one by one: Bohemia, Moravia, and Slovakia. Was Poland next? It seemed likely until the end of March 1939. That is when the British and French promised to defend Poland if the Nazis attacked. The drum beat of war grew louder with each passing day.

appeasement—giving in to another power in order to keep the peace

BLITZKRIEG

Some historians say that the first "soldier" killed during WWII was not in an army. He was actually someone who had been set up to look like a soldier.

The Gestapo was Hitler's secret police. They dressed a prisoner in a Polish army uniform. They took him to the German town of Gleiwitz. The Gestapo shot the prisoner there on the evening of August 31, 1939. Then, Hilter claimed the Polish army had attacked a radio tower in the town.

Lightning War

The Nazis used this invented event as a reason for war. They invaded Poland the next day. German airplanes, tanks, and soldiers swept into Poland in a *blitzkrieg*, or lightning war. Germany's air force was known as the Luftwaffe. They quickly destroyed Poland's air force. German **artillery** pounded Polish cities. The Nazis burned villages. They **executed** Polish peasants and Jews.

The German army moves across Poland on September 1, 1939. ▶

Warsaw Ghetto

The invasion was over by October 6. Germany's blitzkrieg killed or wounded 203,000 Poles. Warsaw is the capital of Poland. The Nazis forced Warsaw's Jews to live in a **ghetto**. The Germans also jailed thousands more Polish Jews in **concentration camps**. Those were places where Jews and others were murdered or forced to work as slaves.

The Soviet Union had secretly signed a treaty with Germany before the invasion. Each side agreed not to attack the other. The Soviets captured the eastern part of the country when the Germans moved into west Poland.

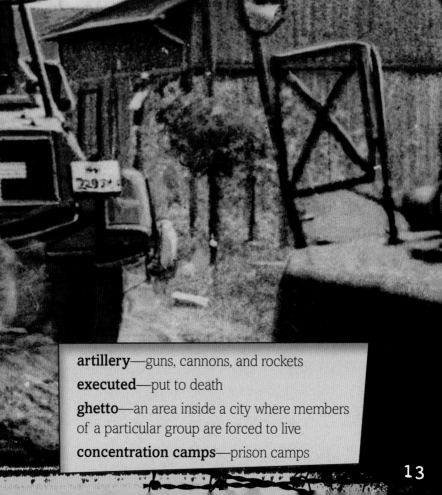

artillery—guns, cannons, and rockets

executed—put to death

ghetto—an area inside a city where members of a particular group are forced to live

concentration camps—prison camps

> Britain and France declared war on Germany on September 3. Neither country was in any position to face down the Nazis.

Poland was now in Nazi hands. Hitler then talked about peace with the Allies. But he was not really willing to settle Germany's differences with Britain or France. Hitler just wanted time for his army to rest and gain strength. Not much happened for several months after Poland fell. Europe settled into a "phony war."

German tanks then raced toward the English Channel in May 1940. This split the combined British and French forces that defended the area. The Germans marched through Europe's lowlands. Meanwhile, a new prime minister took over in Britain. His name was Winston Churchill. He told the nation, "I have nothing to offer but blood, toil, tears, and sweat."

Dunkirk

By May 26, 1940, the Germans had pushed the British and French into a narrow area near Dunkirk. That is a seaport in northern France. Ships of every size set sail from Britain and France. They went to rescue the thousands of Allied troops stuck on the beaches. The **evacuation** was a success.

Battle of Britain

German troops marched into Paris on June 14. France agreed to an **armistice** with Germany on June 22. France had fallen. Great Britain now stood alone. Hitler made plans to invade the island nation. First, Germany's leader wanted his forces to control the air. Then, he planned to start an invasion by sea. The Battle of Britain began in July 1940.

German bombers and fighter planes bombed British factories. They bombed airfields. British fighter pilots bravely fought back. By mid-September, Britain's defense had forced Hitler to delay his invasion. The invasion by sea never came.

Members of a German submarine line up for roll call after returning home from enemy waters. ▶

German bombs destroyed this London railway station.

On June 22, 1941, Germany broke a peace agreement with the Soviet Union. German soldiers, tanks, and aircraft attacked the Soviet Union. They battled along a 2,000-mile-long front.

The Germans code-named the attack "Barbarossa." It was named in honor of Emperor Frederick I Barbarossa. He ruled Germany during the Middle Ages.

Stalingrad

The Nazis swept across the Soviet landscape. By the spring of 1942, the Germans had pressed on toward Stalingrad. That was an important industrial city on the Volga River. Stalingrad was named for Soviet leader Joseph Stalin. The city was also the gateway to an area called the Caucasus. It was rich with oil.

The Soviets Win

The Nazis hoped to capture much-needed oil to fuel their tanks and airplanes. They pushed toward Stalingrad in June and early July. The Soviets defended the city. They fought the Germans in the streets and in buildings.

Stalingrad was in ruins at the beginning of November. The Russians had gained the upper hand by mid-November. The Soviets nearly surrounded 250,000 German troops. The bloody battle continued for two months. The German army finally surrendered on February 2, 1943.

German soldiers fight in Stalingrad.

The Germans' march became bogged down by the Russian winter. ▲

AMERICA AT WAR

In 1940, Japan joined Italy and Germany.
Together, they were known as the Axis
nations. Japan invaded French Indochina
in July 1941. The United States stopped
sending oil to Japan in response.

Pearl Harbor

Japanese and U.S. officials met to discuss ways to find peace. But
Japanese Admiral Isoroku Yamamoto had other plans. He came up
with a secret plan to destroy the U.S. Navy's fleet based in Pearl Harbor,
Hawaii. Yamamoto began his surprise attack on December 7, 1941,
at 7:55 A.M. The Japanese sent 353 airplanes from six aircraft carriers.
Bombs and **torpedoes** rained down on the U.S. fleet.

Declaring War

Five torpedoes ripped through the side of the battleship USS *Oklahoma*.
Hundreds of sailors were trapped below deck. The battleship *Arizona*
exploded. It sank, killing 1,177 Americans on board. More than 2,300
Americans were killed that day. The next day, Roosevelt went before
Congress. He asked for a **declaration** of war.

Congress declared war against Japan the following day. Germany
declared war on the United States on December 11. The United States
went to war against Germany and Italy on December 12.

The Big Three

Great Britain, the United States, and the Soviet Union began to work
together to defeat the Axis nations. Winston Churchill, Franklin Roosevelt,
and Joseph Stalin were known as the "Big Three." The three leaders
would meet several times during the war.

The battleship Arizona *explodes, killing 1,177 sailors and Marines.* ▲

torpedoes—large underwater bombs

declaration—formal announcement

WEAPONS OF WAR

World War II was fought with many new weapons. The new weapons included faster fighter planes, rockets, and aircraft carriers.

Fighters

Fighter planes were smaller and faster than before. They were also deadlier. They could attack quickly and without warning. Bombers moved slowly. It was easy for the fighters to shoot them down. Fighter planes also protected soldiers on the ground. The fighters could shoot enemy soldiers from the air. Often, fighter pilots would battle one another in the air. They called these battles **dog fights**.

New fighter planes, like this P-51 Mustang, took to the skies in WWII. ▲

Floating Airports

The aircraft carrier was one of the most **destructive** weapons of the war. Aircraft carriers were like floating airports. They could carry thousands of men. They could take hundreds of fighter planes and bombers thousands of miles across the ocean.

The Japanese attack on Pearl Harbor highlighted the importance of the aircraft carrier. Much of the war in the Pacific was fought between Japanese and American carriers.

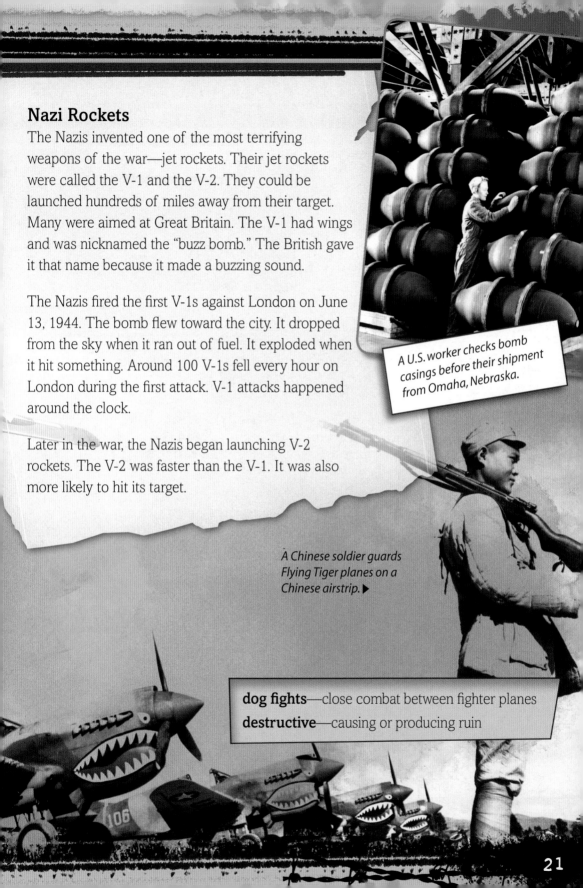

Nazi Rockets

The Nazis invented one of the most terrifying weapons of the war—jet rockets. Their jet rockets were called the V-1 and the V-2. They could be launched hundreds of miles away from their target. Many were aimed at Great Britain. The V-1 had wings and was nicknamed the "buzz bomb." The British gave it that name because it made a buzzing sound.

The Nazis fired the first V-1s against London on June 13, 1944. The bomb flew toward the city. It dropped from the sky when it ran out of fuel. It exploded when it hit something. Around 100 V-1s fell every hour on London during the first attack. V-1 attacks happened around the clock.

Later in the war, the Nazis began launching V-2 rockets. The V-2 was faster than the V-1. It was also more likely to hit its target.

A U.S. worker checks bomb casings before their shipment from Omaha, Nebraska.

A Chinese soldier guards Flying Tiger planes on a Chinese airstrip. ▶

dog fights—close combat between fighter planes
destructive—causing or producing ruin

By 1943, the Allies were fighting to push the Axis out of North Africa and Italy. In the Pacific, the United States battled the Japanese.

Guam, New Guinea, the Solomon Islands, and the Philippines had all fallen to the Japanese. American and Filipino forces defended the Philippine islands as best they could. But they had to **surrender** on April 9, 1942. The Japanese captured almost 78,000 Allied troops. The Japanese forced their prisoners to march to a prison camp. Many U.S. and Filipino soldiers died during the march.

Island Hopping

The Americans had to find a way to battle the Japanese. They came up with a plan called "island hopping." The **strategy** called for American troops to attack and take over one island after another. The troops moved across the Pacific all the way to Japan. The Americans hit the enemy at its weakest points. The Americans won battles at Tarawa, Guadalcanal, and other islands with this strategy.

Major Battles in the Pacific

Bering Sea

Aleutian Islands

OUTER MONGOLIA

MANCHUGO

JAPAN

Areas occupied

CHINA

Hiroshima
Nagasaki

Tokyo

PACIFIC OCEAN

TIBET

Okinawa
(April 1–June 22, 1945)

✱ Iwo Jima
(Feb19–March 26, 1945)

✱ Battle of Midway
(June 4–7, 1942)

TAIWAN

FRENCH INDOCHINA

PHILIPPINES

✱ Saipan (June 15–July 9, 1944)
✱ Guam
(July21–Aug 8, 1944)

South China Sea

✱ Peleliu Palau island
(Sept 15–Nov 27, 1944)

Tarawa ✱
(Nov 20–23, 1943)

Coral Sea

✱ Guadalcanal
(Aug 7, 1942–Feb 9, 1943)

American Marines raise the U.S. flag on top of Mount Suribachi on the island of Iwo Jima.

Midway Island

For a time it looked as though the Japanese would steamroll through the Pacific. Then, they met defeat at the island of Midway. That island is about 1,000 miles northwest of Hawaii. The Japanese tried to destroy the island's defenses. They wanted to force American ships out into the open, where they would be easy to sink. But the Americans broke a secret Japanese code. They discovered the Japanese plan. The U.S. attacked Japan's fleet first and won the battle. From that point on, America was on the **offensive** in the Pacific.

The USS Iowa shows its firepower. ▼

surrender—to give up
strategy—a military plan
offensive—attack made against another force

D-DAY

On June 6, 1944, the Allied invasion of Europe began. It was code-named Operation Overlord. It is better known as D-Day.

The Allies secretly prepared for the invasion. They gathered thousands of ships and troops in Great Britain. The Allies' plan was to cross the English Channel and land on the beaches of Normandy, France. They knew that Normandy was an unexpected place to attack. When the attack began, Hitler believed it was only a **diversion**. He thought the main invasion would come elsewhere. More than 2,800,000 Allied soldiers, sailors, and airmen came ashore, however. They would prove him wrong.

Marching Across Europe

Thousands of Allied forces were moving across France within days. The British and Americans pushed eastward. They **liberated** Paris and the villages and towns along the way. The Russians moved along an 800-mile-long front. It ran from Latvia in the north to Yugoslavia in the south. The Allies were squeezing Hitler's army like a vise.

The Battle of the Bulge

The Allies marched across Belgium late in 1944. Hitler then launched a **counteroffensive**. He tried to force the Allies from the field. The Germans tried to drive a wedge between the Allied armies. The German army used everything at its disposal. That included nearly 1,000 tanks. German troops charged through a wooded area called the Ardennes. They were able to make a bulge in the Allied front lines.

Allied soldiers come ashore in France in 1944. ▶

The Toll Is Taken

The shocked Allies retreated in the freezing cold. Bad weather grounded Allied planes. As the German tanks moved forward, they began to run out of gas. This made them move more slowly. The Allies then counterattacked. The attack was successful. By late January 1945, the Germans had retreated. More than 100,000 Germans had died or were wounded. Allied deaths and injuries totaled 80,000. It was the last of the Germans' great offensives of World War II.

Canadian troops march in France in September 1944.

diversion—a plan used to distract an enemy from a real attack
liberated—set free
counteroffensive—an attack to respond to an enemy attack

THE HOLOCAUST

As the Allies marched across Europe they came across the Nazi death camps.

The Nazis had rounded up Jews long before the war started. The Germans had transported the Jews to concentration camps. At the camps, the prisoners were murdered or forced to work as slaves. It was part of Hitler's "Final Solution" to rid Europe of Jewish people.

Prisoners are freed from a concentration camp in Austria on May 7, 1945. ▼

Experimentation

The Nazis blamed Jews and others for the problems in Germany. The Germans imprisoned millions of Jews and other targets. The camps had names such as Bergen-Belsen, Buchenwald, Auschwitz, Treblinka, and Dachau. Many people were gassed to death. Others were shot or hanged. Nazi doctors experimented on thousands of victims.

Between 1933 and 1945, the Nazis killed many Jews. They also killed non-Jews who opposed the Nazi government. This included many communists. By the end of the war, the Nazis had butchered 11 million people.

Killing the Innocent

In Asia, the Japanese tortured Allied prisoners of war. The Japanese also committed other acts of violence. For example, the Japanese murdered hundreds of thousands of people in Nanking, China. This happened in 1937. When the war ended, the Allies would put Nazi and Japanese officials on trial for these war crimes.

VICTORY

The end of the war was near in April 1945. Soviet soldiers advanced on Berlin. The Americans and British pushed from the west.

Hitler took his own life while deep inside the **bunker** that protected him on April 30. German General Alfred Jodl surrendered on May 7. The Allies would later hang him for war crimes. The war in Europe was over.

The Allies greeted the news with great joy. Winston Churchill reminded the British that they "were the first … to draw the sword against **tyranny**." He said that future generations would look at Great Britain with a sense of awe.

Pacific Theater

The war continued in the Pacific despite victory in Europe. In early 1945, Allied commanders drew up plans to invade Japan. U.S. officials feared, however, that hundreds of thousands of people would die in the attack. Then, there was a change in leadership. President Franklin Roosevelt died in April. His vice president was Harry S. Truman. The vice president had to take over. Truman had to make the biggest decision of his life and of the 20th century.

This photo shows what it looked like after the first nuclear blast over Hiroshima. ▶

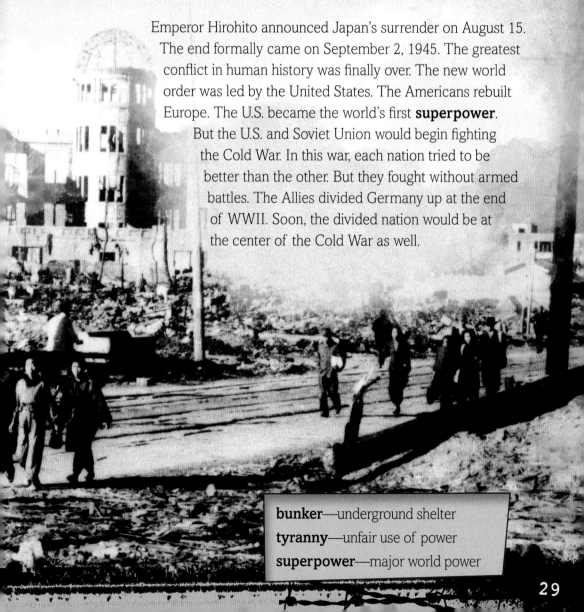

The A-Bomb and Beyond

U.S. scientists had secretly tested the world's first atomic bomb. The "A-bomb" was more powerful than any other kind. U.S. officials hoped that using A-bombs would bring the Japanese to their knees. President Truman gave the order to use the new bombs on Japan. A B-29 bomber called *Enola Gay* dropped the first one on August 6, 1945. It fell on the city of Hiroshima. The bomb exploded in a giant mushroom cloud. Almost 80,000 people died instantly. The Americans dropped a second atomic bomb on the city of Nagasaki three days later.

Emperor Hirohito announced Japan's surrender on August 15. The end formally came on September 2, 1945. The greatest conflict in human history was finally over. The new world order was led by the United States. The Americans rebuilt Europe. The U.S. became the world's first **superpower**. But the U.S. and Soviet Union would begin fighting the Cold War. In this war, each nation tried to be better than the other. But they fought without armed battles. The Allies divided Germany up at the end of WWII. Soon, the divided nation would be at the center of the Cold War as well.

bunker—underground shelter
tyranny—unfair use of power
superpower—major world power

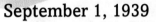

September 1, 1939
Nazi forces invade Poland

September 3, 1939
France and Britain declare war against Germany

April 9, 1940
Norway and Denmark fall to the Germans

May 10, 1940
Germany invades the Netherlands, Luxembourg, and Belgium

June 4, 1940
British and French troops evacuate Dunkirk

June 14, 1940
Paris falls

June 22, 1941
Germany invades the Soviet Union

December 7, 1941
Japanese attack the U.S. at Pearl Harbor, Hawaii

December 8, 1941
United States declares war on Japan

December 11, 1941
The United States declares war on Germany and Italy

January 2, 1942
The Philippines fall to the Japanese

June 3-6, 1942
U.S. victory at the Battle of Midway puts an end to Japan's eastward offensive

February 2, 1943
German troops surrender to the Soviets after three months of fighting at Stalingrad

June 6, 1944
Allies invade Normandy, France

December 16, 1944
Germans counterattack. It begins the Battle of the Bulge

May 7, 1945
Germany surrenders

August 6, 1945
U.S. drops the atomic bomb on Hiroshima, Japan. The U.S. drops a second bomb on Nagasaki, August 9

August 14, 1945
Japan surrenders

INDEX